Welcome to the Spookiest Coloring Adventure! 🎃 👻

Get ready to bring some of the spookiest, silliest, and coolest Halloween scenes to life with your colors! 🖍️ ✨

But wait... there's a twist! 🧙 Along the way, you'll face spooky math challenges—don't worry, they're more fun than fright! 🎃 👻

From sneaky spiders to tricky pumpkins, you'll use your coloring skills and your clever brain to solve the puzzles.

So grab your crayons, sharpen your brainpower, and let's dive into a world of ghosts, goblins, and ... MATH! 🧛 💀

Ready to start?

Flip to the back of the cover to find your spooky color palette and let the fun begin!

10- Brown	17- Green	22- Silver
14- White	18- Yellow	
15- Black	20- Orange	

1- Green	3- Blue	5- Red
2- Violet	4- Brown	

10 & 24- Gray　　**18- Green**
12 & 16 & 28- Brown　**22- Blue**
14 & 20- Beige

10- Black	16- Red	22- Beige
12- Brown	18- Yellow	24- Gray
14- Blue	20- Orange	

10- Purple	17- Brown
12- Blue	19- Gold
15- Gray	22- Silver

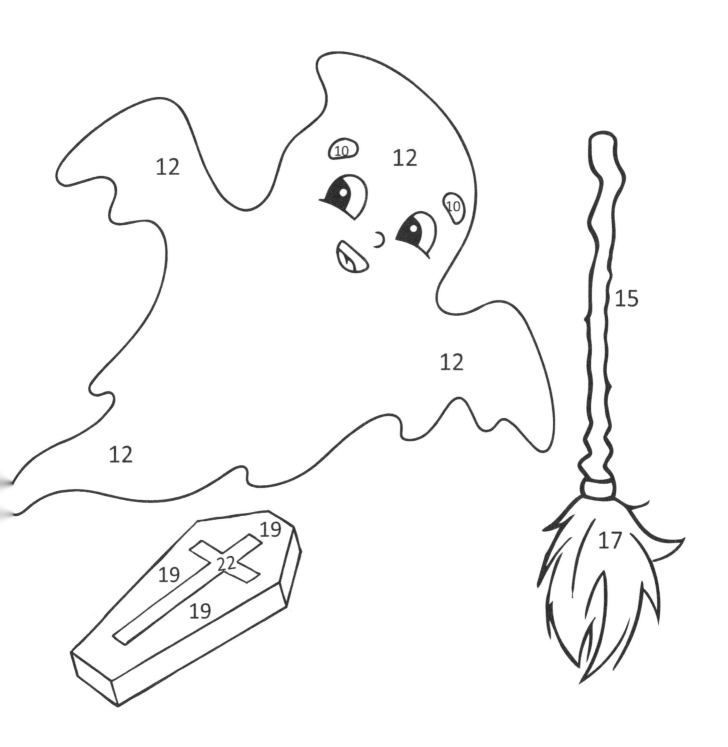

10 & 28- Red   16- Yellow

12- Black   20- Green

14 & 18- Brown   22 & 24- Orange

26- White

30- Violet

10- Beige	16- Pink	22- Gray
12- Brown	18- Yellow	24- Black
14- Red	20- Orange	

10 & 14- Orange
12 & 16- Green

1- Yellow	4- Violet
2- Dark Green	5- Pink
3- Blue	

1- Blue	4- Orange
2- Dark Blue	5- Green
3- Red	

1- Yellow	4- Violet
2- Green	5- Pink
3- Blue	

1- Pink
2- Yellow
3- Blue
4- Green
5- Violet

1- Pink	4- Green
2- Yellow	5- Violet
3- Blue	

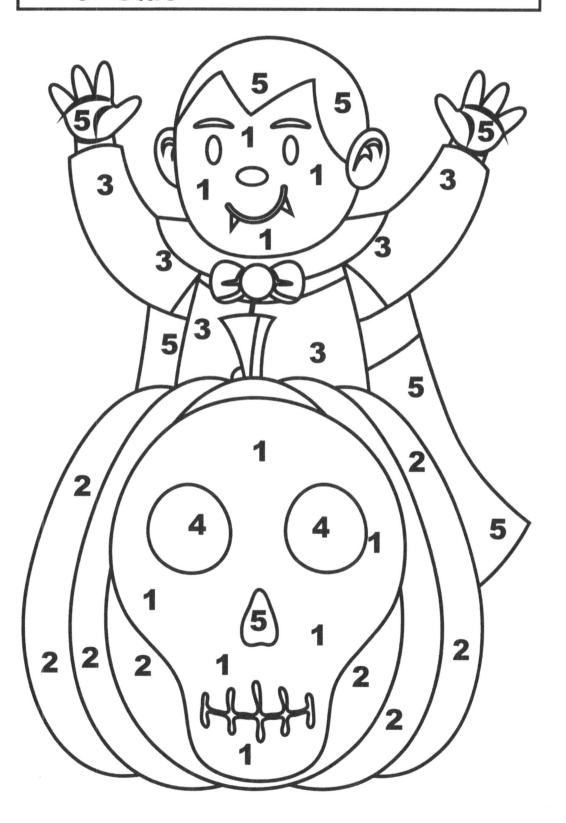

1- Green	4- Gold
2- Violet	5- Red
3- Dark Blue	

1- Green	4- Violet
2- Pink	5- Orange
3- Dark Blue	

1- Green	4- Dark Blue
2- Violet	5- Yellow
3- Blue	

1- Blue	4- Green
2- Red	5- Dark Blue
3- Violet	

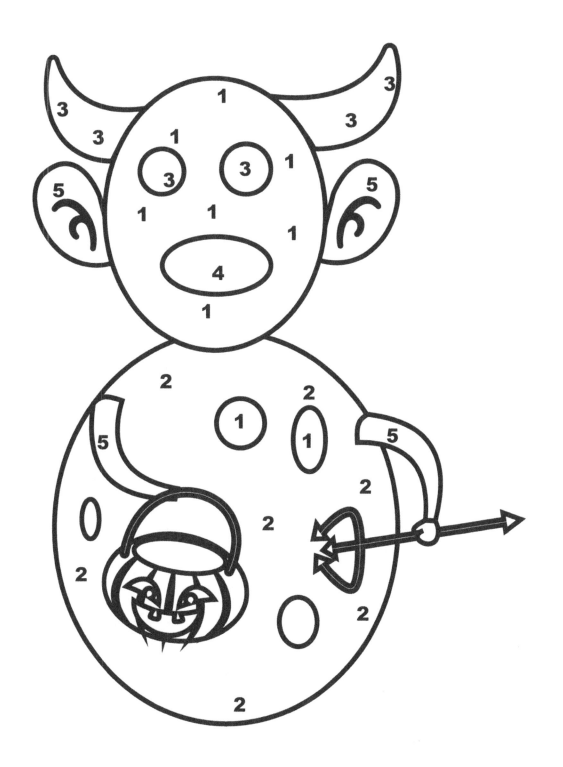

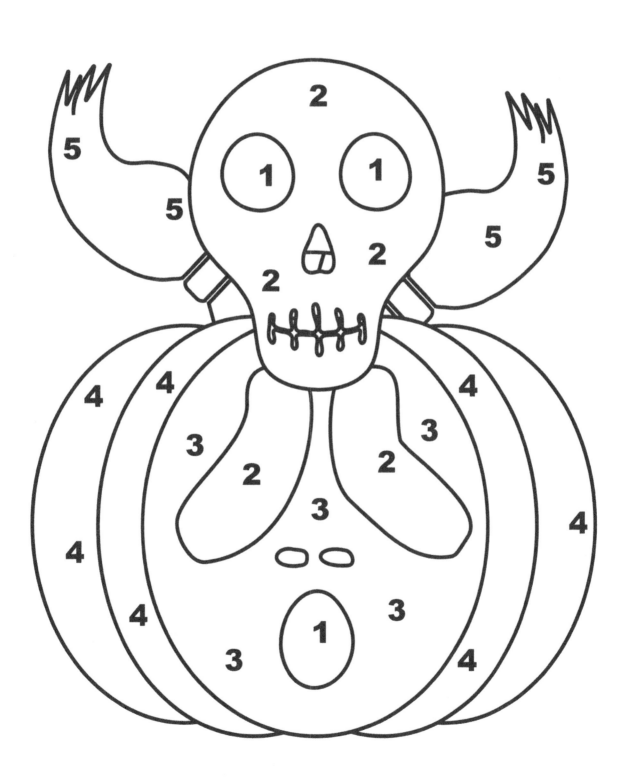

1- Yellow	4- Violet
2- Red	5- Pink
3- Blue	

1- Gray	4- Blue	8- Pink
2- Brown	5- Dark Blue	9- Orange
3- Dark Green	6- Violet	
	7- Red	

1- Dark Gray	4- Green	8- Beige
2- Gray	5- Orange	2- Orange
3- Brown	6- Blue	
	7- Red	

COLOR BY NUMBER : SUBTRACTION

| Green | 6 | Yellow | 5 | Red | 4 |
| Brown | 3 | Orange | 2 | Purple | 1 |

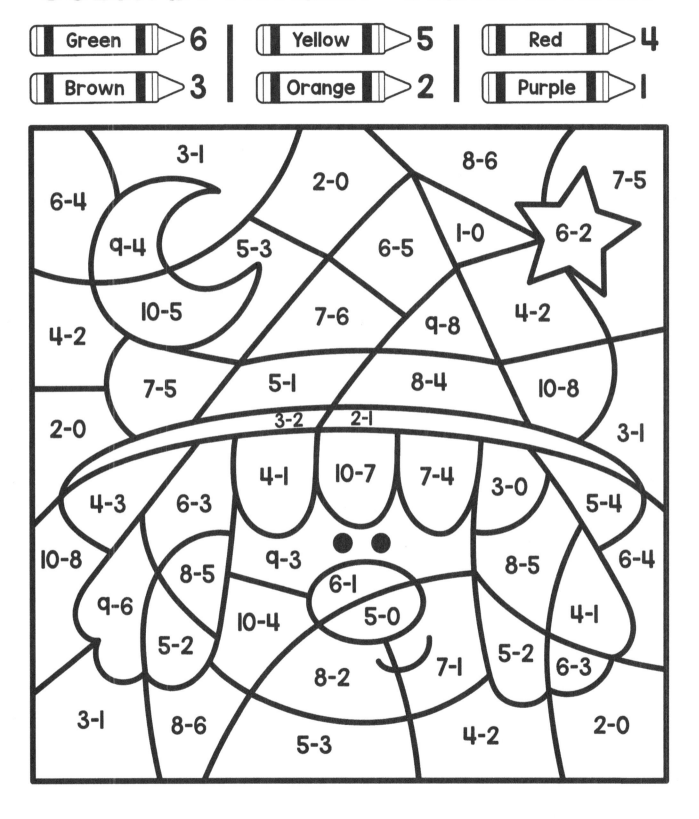

COLOR BY NUMBER : SUBTRACTION

Dark Blue ⟹ 7 | Yellow ⟹ 6 | Brown ⟹ 5
Purple ⟹ 4 | Orange ⟹ 3 | Light Blue ⟹ 2

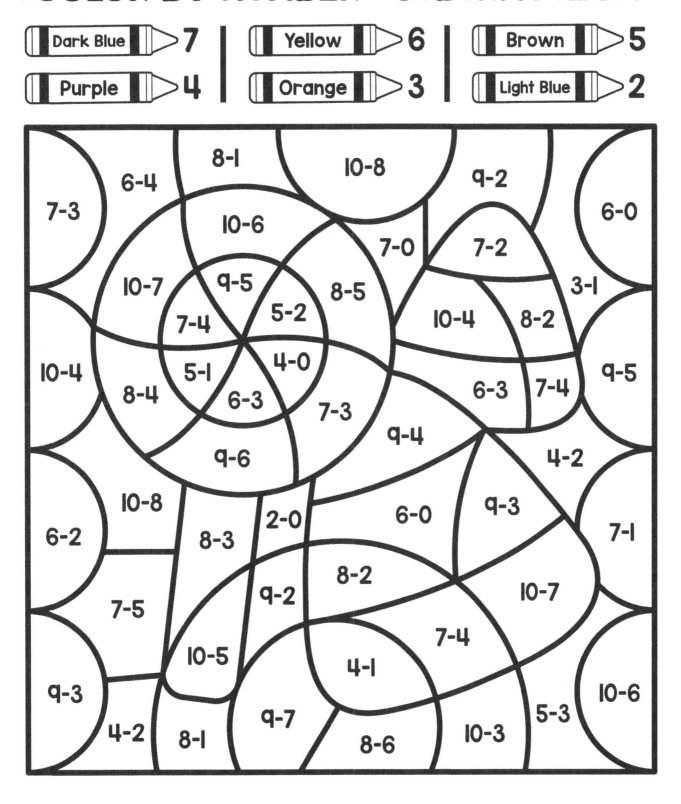

COLOR BY NUMBER : SUBTRACTION

Green ▷ 2 | Black ▷ 3 | Orange ▷ 4
Blue ▷ 5 | Yellow ▷ 6 | Purple ▷ 7

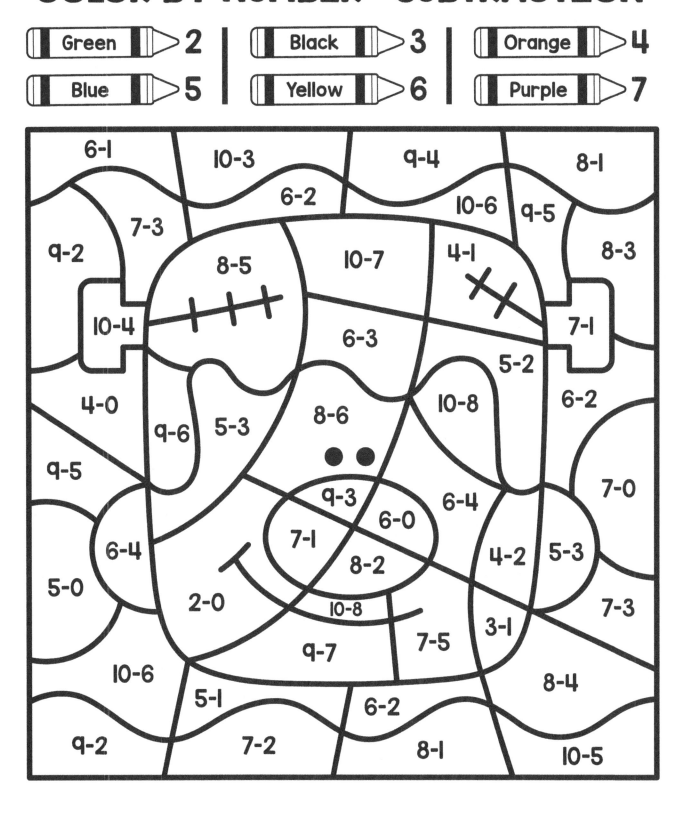

COLOR BY NUMBER : ADDITION

Purple ▷ 10 | Yellow ▷ q | Black ▷ 8

Pink ▷ 7 | Green ▷ 6 | Red ▷ 5

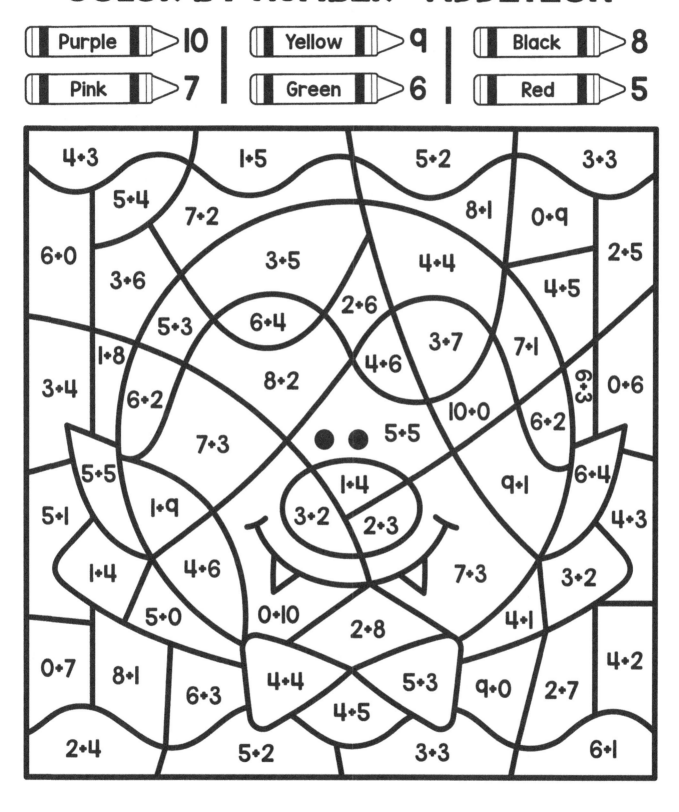

COLOR BY NUMBER : ADDITION

Purple ▷ 10 | Black ▷ 9 | Pink ▷ 8
Yellow ▷ 7 | Green ▷ 6 | Orange ▷ 5

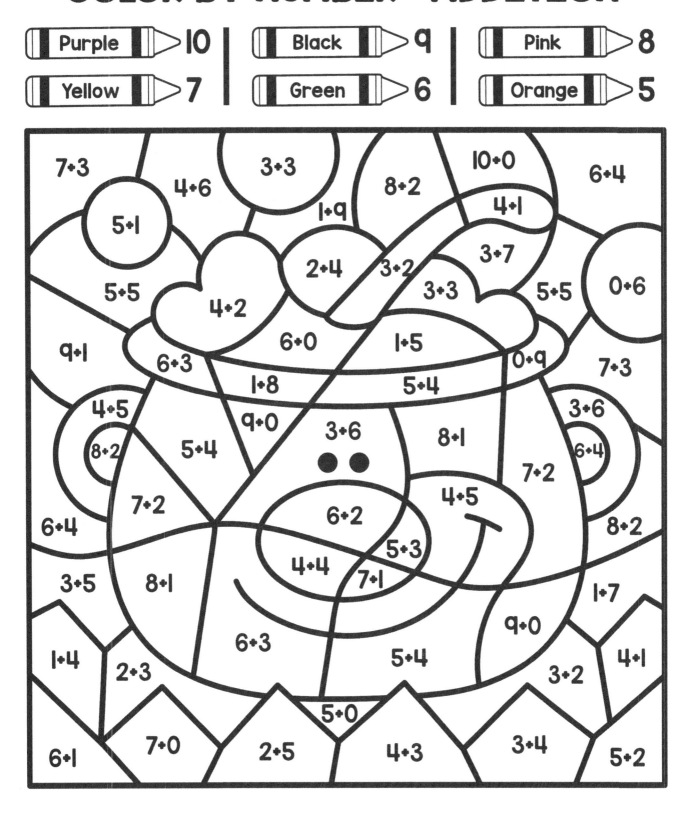

COLOR BY NUMBER : ADDITION

Yellow ▷ 10   Orange ▷ 8   Green ▷ 7
Black ▷ 6   Purple ▷ 5   Blue ▷ 3

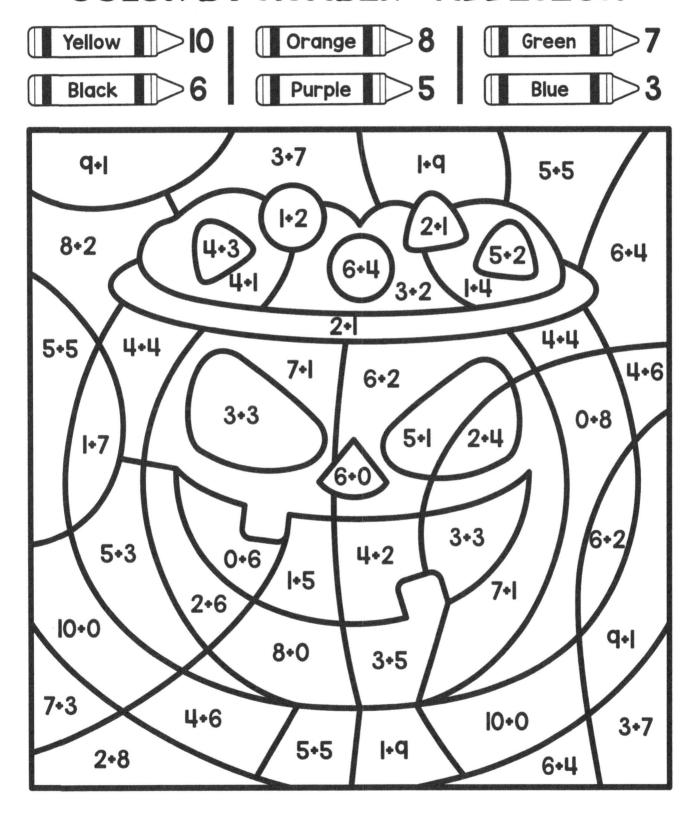

Love Halloween Fun? Check Out Our Next Adventure!

Ready to explore Halloween traditions from around the world? Don't miss "Global Spooky Traditions: A Halloween Activity Book"—a thrilling journey packed with puzzles, coloring, and awesome facts from countries like Mexico, Japan, and Ireland! 🕸️

Perfect for curious kids who want to learn and play, this book is full of spooky fun that will keep you entertained at home or on the go! Grab your copy today and let the global Halloween adventures begin! 🎉 👻

Made in the USA
Las Vegas, NV
16 October 2024

97005384R00050